On Top of Mount Everest

...eries About the Human Body

On Top of Mount Everest

and Other Explorations of Science in Action

Jack Myers, Ph.D.
Senior Science Editor
HIGHLIGHTS FOR CHILDREN

Illustrated by John Rice

Boyds Mills Press

Photo credits: page 27—NASA; page 35—Bill Redic.

Illustration and graphic artwork credits: page 18—based on a figure in T. C. Hsu (1948); page 22—based on J. B. West (1984); pages 23, 45—Jim Postier; page 25—based on a photograph from *High Life* by J. B. West, ©1998 by the American Physiological Society and used by permission of Oxford University Press, Inc.; pages 37, 38—based on figures in A. T. Bahill and T. LaRitz; page 47—based on data from the American Academy of Otolaryngology-Head and Neck Surgery; page 50—based on data from second paper by E. C. Hammond and D. Horn (1958); page 54—based on data from the National Health Interview Survey of the Centers for Disease Control and Prevention.

Published by Boyds Mills Press, Inc.
A Highlights Company
815 Church Street
Honesdale, Pennsylvania 18431
Printed in China
Visit our Web site at www.boydsmillspress.com

Library of Congress Cataloging-in-Publication Data

Myers, Jack.
  On top of Mount Everest: and other explorations
of science in action / Jack Myers ; illustrated by John Rice.
      p. cm.
  Includes bibliographical references and index.
  ISBN 1-59078-252-6 (alk. paper)
  1. Body, Human—Miscellanea—Juvenile literature. 2. Human
physiology—Miscellanea—Juvenile literature. 3. Rice, John. I. Title.

  QP37.M937 2005
  612—dc22

  2004010779

First edition, 2005
The text of this book is set in 13-point Berkeley.

10 9 8 7 6 5 4 3 2 1

CONTENTS

Introduction

Science is the search for understanding of our world. All the fun and excitement is in the search. That's where the action is. That's why this series of books is called Science in Action. It tells about explorations and discoveries as they happened.

All of these explorations have appeared in *Highlights for Children*. Earlier they were called Science Reporting. That was also a good title because most are based on original and current reports cited on page 62. In some cases, new findings were made since my account was published in *Highlights*. I have updated and revised them as needed.

The illustrations are by John Rice. At the beginning of most chapters, he has slipped in just-for-fun illustrations to tell something about the ideas of the articles. Then his main illustrations will help you think about the questions that the scientists asked.

In some books in this series, we have focused on several animals and how each of them handles the special problems of its environment. This book is about just one animal, *Homo sapiens*—that's us, several billions of us. In this book, we look at how we manage in many different environments. Please follow me in the track of the scientists who made the discoveries.

Welcome to Science in Action.

Jack Myers

Jack Myers, Ph.D.
Senior Science Editor
Highlights for Children

Why Do We Laugh?

Seriously . . . why do people chuckle?

You can hear it from people all over the world, no matter what language they may speak. Babies laugh long before they can talk. It's not something you learn in school or from your parents. Laughter must be something that is programmed and built in, a part of what we call human nature.

We usually think of laughter together with humor—a response to something funny. And we know that laughter also works the other way. Things seem funnier when someone else is laughing. Radio and TV shows seem funnier when a background recording of laughter is played at the right times. And you may have seen people break out laughing just from seeing someone else doing it. That's another characteristic that tells us laughter is a built-in part of us.

A Fresh Look

So what can we possibly learn by studying laughter? A scientist who did study it began by thinking about laughter in a new way.

He imagined that he was an alien visiting Earth from another planet to study people. He watched how people behave. He tried to understand a strange part of their behavior called laughter. He studied how people laugh, why they laugh, and how they use laughter in their lives.

That's the way scientists study behavior in wild animals. They ask the same kinds of questions about birds and their songs. The scientist who studied laughter, Dr. Robert Provine, realized that we know more about bird songs than about human laughter.

Ha-ha-ha!

Just as one might do in studying bird songs, Dr. Provine studied the sound pattern of laughter. He found that each person has a characteristic laugh. Women's laughter is usually higher pitched than that of men.

But we all have a common laugh pattern. We make the *ha-ha-ha* sounds all in one breath and while we are breathing out. The

first *ha*'s are louder, and the last are weaker, as if we are running out of breath.

The *ha*'s come in a nice rhythm, about five in a second. It's hard to change that simple pattern. If you purposely try to change the pattern, you will discover how standard and automatic your laugh really is.

Checking out other animals showed that none of them laughs the way people do. The closest is the chimpanzee, which makes laughlike sounds when tickled. But chimpanzee laughter seems more like panting because there is only one *ha* with each breathing-in and each breathing-out. Real laughter is special for humans.

A Serious Side

How do people use laughter in their lives? You already know part of the answer. We don't laugh very often when we are alone. Laughter is something we use socially, when we are interacting with another person, or in groups.

To find out more, Dr. Provine trained his students at the University of Maryland, Baltimore County, to listen in on laughter and find how it is used. The students listened in on 1,200 group conversations in public places, such as schools, malls, and college campuses.

What they learned was a surprise. Most laughter did not come after jokes. It happened just as a part of conversation. In fact, it came from the speaker even more often than from the listeners. And it usually came at the end of a sentence.

They found that people often use laughter in almost the same way we use punctuation in writing—like a period or a question mark. Laughter is sprinkled in between sentences to separate ideas and to make some ideas stand out.

When we use laughter, what message are we giving? You may have noticed we use laughter in two different ways. Sometimes we use it to laugh *at* someone, to make fun of them. To me, that has always seemed unfair—like hitting someone who is already down.

Laughing Together

More often we laugh *with* someone. Then it's a way of showing approval or agreement, that we are thinking alike. Laughter is a part of the way we communicate.

Dr. Provine's study has taught us interesting things about something so common that most of us have never thought about it. There is still a lot to be learned, such as why laughing is so contagious.

Most of what Dr. Provine learned came from watching and listening to people. You and I can do that, too. It's like bird-watching, except that people are more fun.

Can You Roll Your Tongue?

Tongue gymnastics are not for everyone.

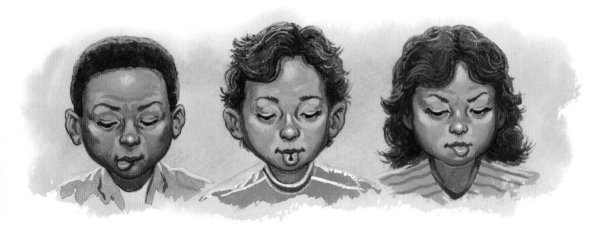

Look in a mirror. Stick out your tongue. Now roll up the sides to form a **U**. What you are trying to do is called *tongue rolling*.

There is something specially interesting about this. It is one of the ways in which our bodies are not all alike. Some people can roll their tongues and some can't. A few people can learn to do it a little after a lot of practice, but for most of us the answer is either yes or no.

Tongue rolling seems to be, at least partly, an inherited characteristic—something each of us inherits from our parents. I first learned about tongue rolling in a letter from four readers of *Highlights for Children* from the Grandview Elementary

School in Indianapolis. It seemed clear that they knew more about tongue rolling than I did. So I went to work to find out about it.

Fortunately, I had a good friend, Dr. C. P. (Pete) Oliver, who had spent his life studying genetics, and especially human genetics. Genetics is the science of inheritance, so Pete was just the right scientist to help me. He had not studied tongue rolling, but he knew where to find studies about it.

Tongue rolling was first studied by a famous geneticist, Professor A. H. Sturtevant, in 1940. Scientists had learned a lot about how inheritance works in plants and animals and were searching for inherited characteristics in people. In a group of 282 people, Dr. Sturtevant found 183 who could roll their tongues and were counted as positives (+) for tongue rolling. The other 99 could not and were counted as negatives (-). Each group had about the same number of men and women. Tongue rolling also seemed to run in families. So Professor Sturtevant reported that about 65 percent of people are positive for tongue rolling and that the condition is at least partly inherited.

Other scientists did more studies to check. One way to ask questions about human genetics is to study identical twins. The idea is that identical twins are special because they develop from a single fertilized egg. That means they start out alike in everything they inherit from their parents.

Two studies have been done on a total of sixty-one pairs of identical twins. Here are the total results:

Both twins can (++) 33	
Neither twin can (--) 13	
One can, one cannot (+-) 15	

You can see that most twins were alike. But in some pairs of identical twins, the two were not alike. This result is taken to mean that tongue rolling is partly determined by inheritance but also partly determined by other factors that we do not know about.

Like many other characteristics in people, tongue rolling must be partly inherited and partly determined by other things that happen to us as we grow up. Maybe some of us exercise our tongues more than others do.

I wondered about tongue rolling in our family and checked all of us. My wife and I can't—we are negative (-). Of our four girls, Kathy, Linda, and Shirley are negative (-), but Jackie is positive (+).

Fancier Tongue Gymnastics

After *Highlights* published the article, I began to hear more about the things some people can do with their tongues. It started with the following letter from Christi Johnson.

"I can do something that no one else I know can do. I can put my tongue in the shape of a three-leaf clover. I thought maybe you could find out if anyone else can do it and have a story on it. I'll try to draw a picture of it."

I agree with Christi. Putting your tongue in the shape of a three-leaf clover is a lot fancier than just rolling up the sides to form a **U**. So I read some more to find what else was known. In studying tongue rolling, scientists noticed that some people, like Christi, could do fancier things with their tongues. Altogether, these fancy things have been called *tongue gymnastics*.

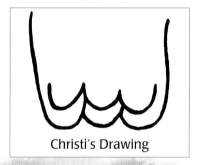

Christi's Drawing

One special tongue movement is called *folding*. This means bending the tip of the tongue upward so that it folds back on itself. Another special form is called the *cloverleaf* tongue. An illustration in the *Journal of Heredity* looked something like this:

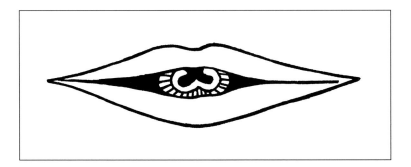

I think this looks like what Christi can do.

I found one study that was made on the tongue gymnastics of 865 people. Of these, 616 could roll their tongues to make a **U**. Of the 616 rollers, 22 could also form a cloverleaf. But no one could fold up the tongue and also make a cloverleaf.

I guess Christi does have an unusual ability because it seems that only about 25 people in 1,000 can make a cloverleaf with their tongues.

I searched but could not find recent studies of tongue rolling. Evidently it is not tied closely enough to inheritance. There are other characteristics, such as people's blood groups, that are completely determined by inheritance. You belong to one of four blood groups that are labeled A, B, AB, and O, and there is nothing you can do to change your blood group. But many human characteristics, like tongue rolling, are only partly determined by our genetic code.

On Top of Mount Everest

It's hard to catch your breath.

Mount Everest rises 29,028 feet above sea level, the highest place on Earth. For people who like to climb mountains, it is special just because it's the highest mountain there is.

Very few people try to climb Mount Everest all alone. It is the highest of the Himalayas, a great range of mountains north of India and in the hard-to-get-to country of Nepal. So climbing Mount Everest takes a large party of people with lots of supplies and careful planning. Long ago, the Sherpas, people who live near the base of the mountains, became guides and carriers for mountain-climbing expeditions.

The usual plan is to make a number of camps, each one higher up the mountainside than the last one. First there is a base camp. Most of the people involved in the expedition live at the base camp and work at carrying supplies to higher camps. Each camp must be in some protected place. The camp provides food and shelter from blizzards that often rage across the mountainside. Finally, very high up, is the last camp. There, two or three of the strongest and best climbers will wait for good weather and will try to reach the top.

The First Climbers

The first well-organized effort to climb to the top was made in 1922. Two of its climbers got within 2,000 feet of the summit, but they were turned back by bad weather. In the next thirty years, seven other teams tried and failed. Finally, in 1953, a British party made it. Edmund Hillary of New Zealand and Tenzing Norgay, a Sherpa, reached the summit. Since then about

one thousand people have stood at the top of Mount Everest, and more than 160 have died trying the climb.

In 1981 an American Medical Research Expedition went to Mount Everest. Five members of the party reached the summit. But the main purpose was to study the human body and how well it works at high altitude. The party had six men with past experience climbing in the Himalayas. It also had six "climbing scientists," all of them doctors with experience in mountain climbing. In addition, there were eight other scientists and forty-two Sherpas.

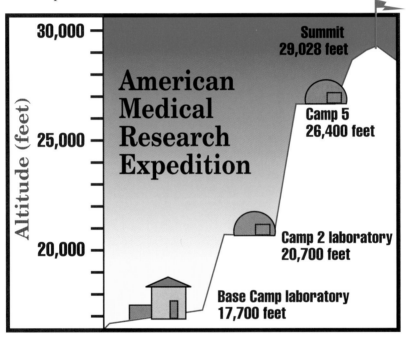

The main problem of high altitude is that the air pressure is so low. That means the air is thin and low in all its gases, including oxygen. At low altitude, where most of us live, getting oxygen out of the air is no problem. Our breathing is under an automatic control, so we don't even have to think about it. Down in the chest, blood passes through little tubes around the air sacs of our lungs. Our breathing rate must keep enough oxygen in the air of the lungs. Then the blood gets a full load of oxygen as it passes through.

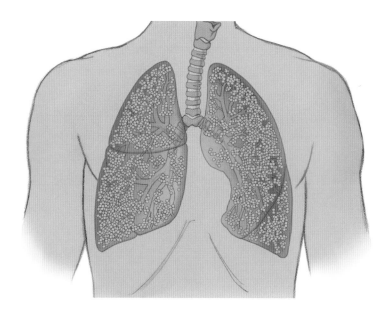

The lungs are full of tiny air sacs, shown here. These sacs are surrounded by tiny tubes (not shown), which carry blood close to the surface of each sac. At this surface, the blood takes up oxygen from the air we breathe in while it also gets rid of the waste gas, carbon dioxide.

When you exercise, your muscles use up oxygen faster. By running fast, you can increase your oxygen uptake about ten times. Then your heart pumps blood faster, and you breathe faster and more deeply. This makes everything work so well that the blood still gets a full load of oxygen as it passes through the lungs.

But at 29,000 feet, getting the oxygen into your blood becomes a problem. The automatic control speeds up the rate of breathing, but there is no way to get quite enough oxygen.

One of the "climbing scientists" who reached the summit took a sample of the air in his lungs. Actually, he caught a sample of his breath, right at the end of an outward breathing, in a tiny vacuum bottle. Then the bottle was brought home for analysis. The sample had only about one-third as much oxygen as a sample taken in the same way at sea level. He was breathing hard and getting lots of outside air into his lungs. Even so, the oxygen in his lungs was so low that his blood never could get enough oxygen, actually less than one-third of a full load.

How fast can the body work when it is getting so little oxygen? Not very fast. A bicycle-like exercise machine was carried up to the laboratory at Camp 2. Experienced climbers were tested while breathing air lower in oxygen, like air at the summit. They could work only about as fast as a person walking slowly at sea level.

Carrying Air

Mountain climbing is hard work. You can see why most climbers high on Mount Everest carry small tanks of oxygen to help their breathing. About one hundred climbers have made it to the top without carrying oxygen, but those were extreme tests of courage and endurance. The first two who climbed Everest without oxygen recalled that, near the top, they could climb only about 6 feet in a minute. They were close to the limit of getting enough oxygen to stay alive.

The medical team asked a lot of other questions. Some of them are still without answers. One result was very clear. The best climbers at very high altitudes are those who can breathe best and get air fastest to their lungs when they exercise. As in many sports, some people have more natural ability than others. Still, better breathing is something to work on if you want to be a mountain climber.

Living High Up

The Mount Everest expedition was one of several high-altitude scientific expeditions. A high mountain provides a laboratory for studying how the body responds to the special stress of low oxygen. In 1935, an earlier expedition had gone to the Andes Mountains in Chile, where a railroad goes almost all the way to a sulfur mine on Mount Aucanquilcha at 19,000 feet. The miners were native people who lived in the mining camp of Quilcha at 17,500 feet, the highest "town" in the world. A report of the expedition made a big thing of the daily routine of the miners. Every evening they returned to Quilcha to spend the night. They chose to make the hard climb every morning—which took an hour and a half—rather than live continuously at the higher altitude. So those miners were often quoted as holding the record for living at highest altitude.

Dr. John West wondered how high up people really can live. He had been a member of the Mount Everest expedition, and he had noticed that in their living hut at 19,000 feet most members of the party continued to lose weight during their five-month stay, even though they ate carefully prepared diets and had a healthy exercise program. Out of curiosity, he went to Chile in 1985 to check out the miners living there at high altitude. He was astonished to find four men living right at the mine as caretakers. One man had been living there for two years. They all got a break once a week, on Sundays, when a truck took them to Amincha to see their families and play soccer.

Even in the high-up places of the world—like Nepal and Tibet of Asia or the Andes Mountains of South America—few people choose to live above 15,000 feet, where it's so hard to breathe. Thanks to Dr. West's curiosity, we have a record of a few who did, the caretakers of the Aucanquilcha mine, who lived at 19,000 feet.

Living in Space

Can we stay healthy in microgravity?

Our astronauts have lived in space for several months, and a few Russians have stayed in orbit for a year or more. They have taught us that life in space is different from life on Earth in many ways. One difference is that out there we are no longer living close to the great mass of Earth and the pull of its gravity that gives us our sense of "up and down." Can we really live without gravity? Sometime before our next big adventure into space, we need an answer to that question.

Actually, there may be no such thing as zero gravity. Even in satellites orbiting Earth, astronauts live in *microgravity*—about a millionth of the pull at Earth's surface. It is so small that there is no feeling of up or down.

Living in microgravity is no picnic. It's no fun to have to hang on just to stay put—or to strap yourself in at night so you will still be in bed in the morning. And gravity is important to the working of your body. On Earth, you seldom have to think about it because it's always there for you. Many of your muscles are working against the effects of gravity most of the time. So you can see why your body might have some problems adjusting to microgravity.

Space Sickness

From studies on astronauts, we know some effects of microgravity. One important effect occurs on the body's balancing system. In adjusting to microgravity, the system gets confused about up and down. About half of all astronauts get space sickness. That's like car sickness and includes all the bad feelings that can lead to vomiting. Fortunately, it usually doesn't last long.

Living in microgravity looks like fun, but it can cause medical problems, too.

A second effect on the body occurs in the blood-supply system. The system already has ways to respond to small changes in effects of gravity. When you are lying down, your body is mostly on the same level. When you stand up, blood naturally tends to run downhill toward your feet. Then your heart works harder to pump blood up to your chest and head. And in your legs, the arteries (the little tubes carrying blood from the heart) are tightened and made smaller by tiny muscles in their walls.

After some time in microgravity, blood shifts toward the chest and head. Coming back to Earth leads to a sudden shift back to the legs and away from the brain. In some astronauts, this has led to a feeling of faintness lasting several days.

There are also some longer-lasting effects. Muscles slowly waste away, as they always do when not being used. Bones have a problem, too. When no longer loaded by the weight of gravity, bones slowly lose calcium minerals and become lighter and weaker.

Space Fitness

Two ways have been found to counter the effects of microgravity. Astronauts returning to Earth wear tightly fitting suits to help keep blood normally distributed. And while they are out in space, astronauts spend several hours a day in exercise. They use exercise machines with springs or bungee cords, or they strap themselves to a stationary bicycle. Exercise provides "loading" for bones and muscles to take the place of effects of gravity on Earth.

We have learned a lot about microgravity, but not enough to know how to manage with it on really long space flights. Any new exploration—like a two- or three-year trip to Mars—will have some unknown dangers. The effects of microgravity on the body may be one of them.

More Troubles for Space Travelers

Besides microgravity, there are other problems for people in space.

Diet

Food on a spacecraft must be prepared in some simple way from dehydrated packages. What should the food be? How should it be fixed so it doesn't taste like cardboard?

Radiation

People will be exposed to greater levels and different types of radiation than we get on Earth. Can we find different diets or drugs to counter effects of radiation?

Body Rhythm

Your body has a sleep-awake rhythm that is neatly adjusted to our night-day cycle on Earth. Any change in the night-day cycle means that the body's rhythm must adjust. We know about a common problem of airline passengers who fly partway around the world. Because their body rhythm is slow to adjust, they have difficulties in sleeping or in just staying awake under a new night-day cycle. How can we help the body adjust its rhythm?

Thinking about all the special health problems of people in space has led to a new approach: The National Space Biomedical Research Institute. It is made up of doctors, scientists, and engineers from twelve universities, working in teams. It is helping us learn how to manage people in space.

Roommates in Space

How will Mars explorers handle the long, dull voyage?

"**W**ho would you choose to go with, cooped up on a space vessel on a trip to Mars?" That's the question Dr. JoAnna Wood asked me when I talked to her about her work at the National Space Biomedical Research Institute.

In space exploration, we always need to be looking ahead. While astronauts are still building the International Space Station, parked in orbit around Earth, we are thinking ahead to the next big push.

That would be a trip to explore Mars. We are a long way from being ready, but space scientists are pretty well agreed on what the trip will be like. The biggest challenge is that it will be the longest space voyage ever taken: a trip of about three months to get there, then maybe a year-long stay to learn about Mars, then another long trip home.

How big a crew will be needed? To study Mars we will need a crew of about six or seven people, each with special knowledge or skills for the exploration.

How much room will they have? About as much as in a big school bus. Of course, it will be better organized for living. But there will be no unused space where anyone can "get away." There will be a lot of togetherness.

If you have a brother or sister, or have shared a bedroom, or have gone with your family on a long car trip, then you may have had a taste of the problem. Not all of us are good at living with a few others in a small space. Living like that takes special effort, even for people who are good at it.

Stress on a Glacier

Dr. Wood wanted to find out how people behave when working in small groups under stressful conditions. Her first study was of two Australian teams of six scientists and engineers (all men) who explored the Antarctic Lambert Glacier, the world's largest glacier, in 1993–1994 and 1994–1995.

Both teams traveled as caravans with bulldozers pulling laboratories and living quarters on sleds. On each team, everyone shared duties like tractor driving and cooking, and they met together once each day. The men could receive faxed written messages from their families but could talk to them only once (at Christmas) by radiotelephone.

So each team had about 110 days of isolation. And team members were always under stress because of the possibility that under the snow there might be a glacier crevasse wide enough to swallow tractors and sleds.

Under the heavy work of exploration, few people want to

spend time writing. So Dr. Wood designed a list of questions that would be easy to answer each week on a computer keyboard. There were seventy-one questions designed to ask each man how he thought he was performing, whether he was happy or depressed, whether he was mentally alert, and whether the team was working well together.

Dr. Wood's study showed large differences among people in how well they managed under stress. One man had such low morale that he was depressed and thought his performance was poor throughout his reports. Another man, who said he had no problems at all, did not know that several men on his team were irritated by him.

More Antarctic Stress

Dr. Wood also studied eight different groups, each of about twenty men and women of the Australian Antarctic Research expeditions of 1996 and 1997. Each party was made up of scientists studying the Antarctic winter and of people who took care of living needs (chefs, doctors, and radio operators). They all lived together in buildings that were designed for blizzards and for -40 degrees Fahrenheit.

These people were not in constant danger. But they were isolated for nearly eight months of almost continuous darkness. Everyone worked at group tasks like kitchen duties, but except for some field trips away from the station, there was a lot of boredom. So in addition to the fast-answer questions, Dr. Wood asked: "Please tell us about any positive (pleasant) or negative (unpleasant) experiences since your last report."

It took lots of work to study all of the reports. The most common response was "nothing to report," but many team members reported both positive and negative experiences. There were many expected negative reports about living conditions (like darkness and bad weather or lack of privacy). There also were many negative reports about "interpersonal" experiences, such as feelings of anger and irritation between individuals.

And there were some easy-to-see differences between groups. In one group, people made many negative reports about the station leader. Another group was distinctive in that its people seemed to get along together so well that they had very few negative interpersonal reports.

Ready for Mars?

Dr. Wood and others she works with have a long way to go in helping us understand the needs of the Mars explorers. When I asked her what she had already learned, she replied, "Of course, the astronauts will have to be chosen for their abilities to explore and study Mars. I think they will be most successful if they also are good at the special needs of teamwork in aiding and supporting each other."

Finally, I asked if she had any special message for young readers. "Yes," she said. "Call me when you're ready."

Why You Can't Keep Your Eye on the Ball

Can an "eye jump" help improve your swing?

Look at the photo on page 35. The man with the baseball bat is a scientist, Dr. Terry Bahill. He is studying how a batter's head and eyes work when hitting a baseball. Most of the study was done with a professional baseball player as the batter, but I am glad we have a photo to show you the scientist himself.

Dr. Bahill has wires going to a lot of gadgets strapped to his head. There are little photocells held by his glasses that catch light reflected by the front surface of his eyes. They can tell the direction his eyes are pointing. There is a stick pointing up from his glasses with a light on top. There also are two other little lights strapped to his head. Up above and out of the photo, a TV camera is taking pictures of the three lights to record the movements of his head.

In front of Dr. Bahill you can see a plastic ball. It is traveling on a string. A second string is being wound up on the pulley of a motor. It pulls the ball at a constant speed from the pitcher's mound to the position of the catcher behind home plate. Counting turns of the motor tells where the ball is at any time. The TV camera and the instruments wired to all those gadgets make a record of the batter's head and eye movements as he watches the ball.

The batter has the problem of tracking the ball so he will know when and where to swing his bat. To track a moving object, your eyes and brain must work together. They can work together fast enough to keep your eyes fixed on a jet plane high in the sky. They work even faster to follow a bird close by.

Now think about tracking a baseball. For the first few seconds after the ball leaves the pitcher's hand, it is easy to track. Because it is coming almost straight toward you, your eyes do not need to move very much. But the closer it comes, the faster your eyes must move.

The diagram on page 37 will show you the idea. The ball comes forward at constant speed. To track it, your eyes must move like the arrow in the diagram. Just like the arrow the angle of the eyes to the ball must increase faster and faster. Can your eyes keep up with the ball?

Let's see how the experiment worked when the batter was a professional ballplayer. The diagram on page 38 shows you the result for a ball thrown at a speed of 60 miles per hour. The solid line shows how the angle of the eyes changed. The dashed line shows how the angle should have changed to keep the eyes on the ball. The two lines go together most of the way, but not all the way. You can see that the batter could keep his eyes fixed

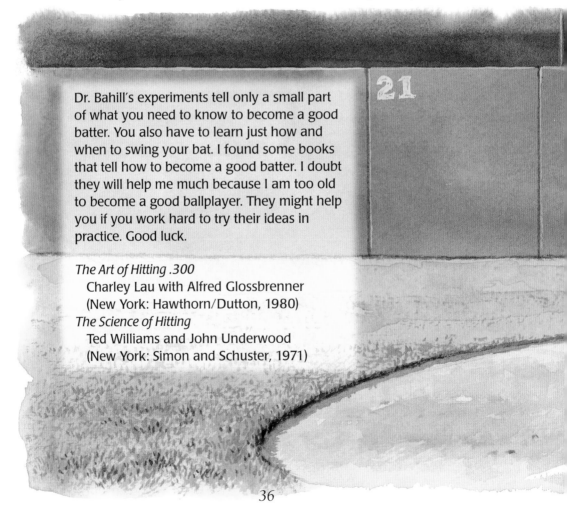

Dr. Bahill's experiments tell only a small part of what you need to know to become a good batter. You also have to learn just how and when to swing your bat. I found some books that tell how to become a good batter. I doubt they will help me much because I am too old to become a good ballplayer. They might help you if you work hard to try their ideas in practice. Good luck.

The Art of Hitting .300
   Charley Lau with Alfred Glossbrenner
   (New York: Hawthorn/Dutton, 1980)
The Science of Hitting
   Ted Williams and John Underwood
   (New York: Simon and Schuster, 1971)

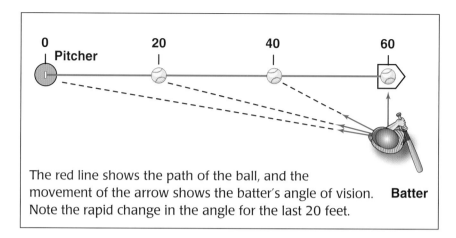

The red line shows the path of the ball, and the movement of the arrow shows the batter's angle of vision. Note the rapid change in the angle for the last 20 feet.

Batter

on the ball until time to start his swing. He could track it until it was about 5½ feet away from the plate. But he could not keep his eyes fixed on the ball all the way to the plate. So he could not see his bat hit the ball.

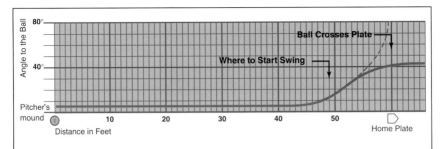

80° ─

Angle to the Ball

40° ─

Pitcher's mound

Distance in Feet

10   20   30   40   50

Ball Crosses Plate

Where to Start Swing

Home Plate

This solid red line shows how quickly a professional ballplayer changes his angle of vision as the ball crosses the plate.

The dashed line shows how the angle of the eye would have to change to keep the eye on the ball at all times.

Dr. Bahill was not surprised by the results. It was known from other studies that a fastball passing a batter requires a change in eye angle much faster than any person can make. However, he also found that the professional ballplayer with lots of training was much better at tracking the ball than some students who tried it.

If you want to see your bat hit the ball, there is a sneaky way to do it. If you want your eyes to sweep across a page—as you are reading now—or across the objects in a room, your eyes always move in little jerks. Eye movements like these are called *saccadic jumps*. You can't use them to follow a moving object because when your eyes jump from one point to another, you do not see anything in between. But there is a way you can use a saccadic jump to see your bat hit the ball.

First you must track the ball long enough to start your swing. Then you purposely make your eyes jump ahead to the place where you think the ball will cross the plate. And then—if you made a good swing—you may get to see your bat hit the ball.

Of course, you can't get a hit just by seeing the ball cross the plate. By that time it is too late to change your swing. However, Dr. Bahill thinks that doing this on purpose in practice might help you learn how your swing is working.

The Sun and Your Skin

You can't see ultraviolet rays,
but they can hurt your skin.

Every year, we look forward to spring. The days get longer, and that big old sun moves higher across the sky. There are lots of sunny days ahead. A great time for playing. A bad time for your skin.

Hidden in all that sunshine is a bad part, a "color" your eye can't see. It's a part of sunlight called ultraviolet rays, or *UV*. It is so damaging that most living things have had to develop some kind of protective cover to screen it out. Your skin protects you by absorbing UV. But while UV might not reach your insides, it can harm your skin.

Just as in many other animals, human skin has some melanin, a dark pigment that is a good absorber of UV. When melanin is close to the skin's surface, it can protect even the skin itself. But our skin color varies widely, so some of us are more sensitive to sun than others. The lighter your skin, the more sensitive it is to the sun's harmful rays.

Sunburn

You might already know about sunburn. You go to the beach or out for a long hike early in the summer. Your skin takes a big dose of sun. That night your skin is red, feels hot, and probably hurts. In a few days, the burn will cool and your skin will feel well again. But deep down there will be a little damage from which your skin will never recover.

You might also know about suntan. That's what happens to many of us if we are exposed to the sun a little at a time. Tanning is the skin's way of trying to protect itself by making more melanin.

A suntan might look nice, but by the time you get one, the deeper layers of skin have been damaged. Some of the supporting protein—*collagen*—is destroyed. Elastic fibers gradually lose the stretchiness that keeps your skin tight and smooth. Though it may happen very gradually over the years, the skin tends to get leathery and wrinkled. So avoid tanning, including sun lamps and tanning beds.

There is one more effect of UV that makes it even worse. Years of exposure to UV can cause skin cancer. Every year more than one million Americans discover that they have some form of skin cancer.

Fortunately, we have ways to protect our skin from UV. The best way is to wear protective clothing like wide-brimmed hats, long sleeves, long pants, and UV-blocking sunglasses.

A second way is to pick the time of day to be outside. That way we can use the earth's atmosphere to screen out UV more completely.

If we did not have the protection of our atmosphere, especially its high-up ozone layer, we would never dare go outside without being completely covered. Sunlight wouldn't look much brighter, but it would have at least 250 times more UV. Even though cutting down on UV by 250 times sounds like a lot, that's still not enough protection.

Now look at the drawing that shows sunlight coming to us on the earth. You will see that, when it comes in at an angle, it must pass through a lot more atmosphere. Then we get more

Here are two paths of sunlight through the atmosphere and its ozone layer. The shorter path, when the sun is directly overhead, gives us the most ultraviolet light. The longer path, when the sunlight is slanted in the morning and afternoon, gives us better protection from the sun's ultraviolet rays.

protection because more UV is absorbed. Now you know why it is common advice to stay out of the summer sun between 10 A.M. and 4 P.M.

There's another way to figure out whether the sun's angle is enough to protect you. Check out the length of your shadow. If your shadow is longer than you are, then the path of sunlight through the atmosphere is long enough to give you reasonable (but not complete) protection.

Sunscreens and Sunblocks

There's a third way to protect yourself from UV: Use a sunscreen. Sunscreens stick to the surface of your skin and absorb UV. A "broad-spectrum" sunscreen works best because it protects against both of the harmful types of UV. (See page 43.) If you choose one that says SPF 15, it will screen out so much UV that getting a sunburn will take fifteen times longer. And if you are going swimming, look for a sunscreen that is waterproof or water-resistant and won't wash away. Some people who are very sensitive choose sunscreens so complete that they are called sunblocks. A danger with these products is that people often count on them too much, stay in the sun too long, and fail to put more on after swimming or toweling off. They actually get more UV exposure than they would have otherwise.

Most sunscreens don't show, and anyone who is smart is already using one. Think of what might happen if you don't use one. It's not too much trouble to brush your teeth—and you get two sets of teeth. But you get only one skin.

If you think you're too young to start worrying about your skin, think again. The younger you are, the longer your skin has to last.

Frequency

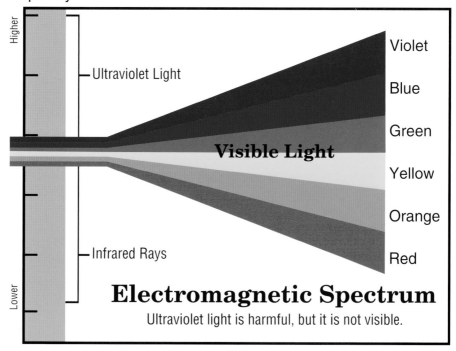

Higher

Lower

Ultraviolet Light

Violet

Blue

Green

Visible Light

Yellow

Orange

Infrared Rays

Red

Electromagnetic Spectrum

Ultraviolet light is harmful, but it is not visible.

Ultraviolet really means "beyond violet," the color at the extreme blue end of the color lineup of the rainbow. Then the ultraviolet is divided up into three parts. UVC is closest to violet. (The eyes of some insects can see it.) A broad band of UVA is farthest away. UVA has so much energy that it is very damaging. It kills little organisms like bacteria and causes wrinkles and cancer in human skin, but there is not much of it in the sunlight we get on the earth. That's why we worry mostly about the in-between band of UVB, which also causes wrinkles and skin cancer.

• Most clouds do not block UV. If the sun is high in the sky, don't trust a cloud to screen it out.

• Glass does block UV. Some car windows may not block much of it, but none of it gets through ordinary window glass.

• Scientists are worried that the ozone layer is getting thinner. That means more UV will be getting through.

Noise and Old Ears

Don't let your ears grow old fast.

I have old ears—they don't hear very well. That's no surprise because I am an older person. But it may surprise you that young people can have old ears, too. Scientists have found that enough exposure to loud sounds can give you ears that are older than your number of birthdays. And that works for sounds you want to hear as well as for background sounds that we call noise.

Your ear is a very sensitive gadget for hearing sounds. The *outer ear* is the only part you can see. It opens into a tube, the *ear canal*, which leads inside and ends in a thin membrane called the *eardrum*. On the other side of the eardrum is an air-filled space called the middle ear. Small bones of the middle ear carry vibrations of the eardrum across to another small membrane of the inner ear. That's a very sensitive place, a little cavity protected by a bony case.

Sound waves in the air cause vibrations of the eardrum. Then those vibrations pass through to the *inner ear*. That's where the action is. There is a lineup of some very special cells, called hair cells because each one has many tiny bristles that look like hair even though they are much smaller. Connecting to them are the endings of nerve cells, which have nerve fibers leading to the brain. Even a little motion of a "hair" sets off a hair cell so that it zaps its nearest nerve ending. That sets up a nerve message.

Of course, there will be nerve messages from many hair cells. When your brain puts together all the nerve messages, you *hear* the sound.

Even though lots of things can go wrong, our ears usually work right all our lives. However, our ears have their own way of growing old. We were born with about 15,000 of those special hair cells in each inner ear. As we go through life, there are times when all of us are exposed to loud noises. A loud noise, particularly one that continues, may destroy some of those hair cells. And once destroyed, they can never work again. It's just

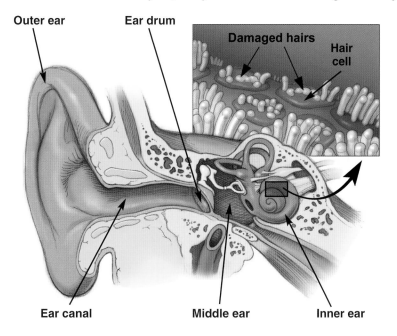

45

that simple: the age of your ears is measured by how many hair cells you have lost. You can see that, with enough noise, your ears can grow old faster than you do.

My reason to tell you all this is not that I want to scare you. That wouldn't help either of us. I'm telling you so you can be careful and take care of your ears. Let's talk about that last part.

Soft Sounds, Loud Sounds

The intensity of loudness of sound is measured on a scale of decibels (dB). The faintest sound heard by the human ear is put at zero (0 dB). The loudest sound a human is likely to hear is close to a rocket launching, about 180 dB. In the table on page 47, you will see estimates for some different kinds of sounds or noise and how long it takes for them to be dangerous. You will see that until they get to be loud, noises never cause any ear damage. For louder noises, the longer you hear them, the worse they are. And for a really loud noise like a gunshot up close, any length of time is too long.

The table is only a rough guide, but it will give you an idea of noises loud enough to be dangerous. You will understand, of course, that any noise gets weaker the farther you get from its source. Even a thunderclap sounds weak if you are far enough away.

What should you do if you can't get away from dangerous noise? Try earplugs made of rubber, foam, or plastic. Many sporting-goods stores have them. Or try the special ear protectors sold by most stores that sell guns. (Plugs of cotton aren't much help.)

How can you tell if a noise is loud enough to be dangerous? Because people differ, there is no exact way to tell. But there is a rather simple rule: If someone has to shout to make you hear over a background noise, then that noise may be dangerous.

What about headphones? That's what started me thinking

Noises and Their Danger to Your Ears

Examples	Danger Time
Weakest sound heard by human ear	No danger
Quiet library, soft whisper	No danger
Normal conversation	No danger
Lawn mower	After 8 hours
Snowmobile	Before 8 hours
In front of speakers at a rock band concert	Within minutes
Rocket launching	Any time at all

0 30 40 50 60 70 80 90 100 120 140 180

Typical Loudness (decibels)

about ears. I noticed that many people seem to like their music loud. I guess you can see that their ears may not be as happy with loud music as they are. Again there is that simple rule: If someone has to shout to get your attention, you have your music turned up too loud.

Now that you know about it, don't let your ears get older than you are.

Science Looks at Smoking

The "disease detectives" measured the dangers of cigarette smoking.

The U.S. Surgeon General's Warning reads: "Smoking Causes Lung Cancer, Heart Disease, Emphysema."

"Everyone knows that."

Yes, but how do you know? Just because someone says so?

"Well, OK, how do we know?"

We know because of the work of a special group of scientists. Let's call them the *disease detectives*, the detectives of the medical world. They search for the causes of disease.

And they have learned how to study other things that affect our health. They have found things in the environment that can be harmful—like asbestos and lead. And they showed why we should wear seat belts in cars.

The Tobacco Question

Of all the great work of the disease detectives, I think the greatest was in proving that cigarettes are bad for our health.

Forty years ago doctors *thought* that smoking was one of the causes of cancer, bronchitis, and heart attacks. But that wasn't good enough for evidence. Some nonsmokers also get these diseases, and some smokers live to old age without any signs of disease. So how do you prove that cigarette smoking causes disease—especially when the tobacco companies and their ads are trying to get people to smoke?

Another problem with studying the dangers of cigarette smoking is that the same effects may also be caused by other factors. For example, we know that eating a lot of fatty foods can increase a person's chances of getting heart disease. And we know that air pollution can give us higher chances of getting lung cancer.

So the job for the disease detectives was clear. They needed to study a large number of people who were as alike as possible except that some were smokers and some were nonsmokers.

Such a huge study would be a challenge. Disease detectives at the American Cancer Society took it on.

The Greatest Hunt

The hunt for the killer was the greatest ever. For a period of almost four years, the scientists kept records on 187,783 men.

Some of the men were smokers, and some were nonsmokers. They lived in many different parts of the country, from farms to cities, which often have dusty or polluted air.

For each man who died, the disease detectives obtained medical records to find the cause of death. To see the effects of smoking, they compared the numbers of deaths of smokers to those of nonsmokers.

But there was another problem: Older people die at a higher rate than younger people do. The disease detectives had to show the effects of smoking and not aging. So they compared smokers only with nonsmokers of the same age.

Finally, when all the numbers were in, they laid out the results.

DEATHS

This graph compares the chances of dying in a year for two groups of people: moderate smokers of cigarettes and nonsmokers. In other words, who dies faster (and younger), smokers or nonsmokers? If we kept records on a group of smokers and an equal-sized group of nonsmokers, then 170 smokers would die for every 100 nonsmokers who die.

Died of lung disease

Died of cancer

Died of diseases of heart & circulatory system

Died of other causes

Nonsmokers

100
2
16
62
20

Moderate smokers of cigarettes

170
5
31
109
25

There are different ways to look at the results. One way is shown by the graph. Here's what it says: If there were just as many smokers as there are nonsmokers, then for every 100 nonsmokers who died, there would have been 170 moderate cigarette smokers who died. So you can also say the chances of dying in a year increased by 70 percent for these cigarette smokers.

How much people smoked also affected their chances of death. Those who smoked less each day had a smaller increase in their chances of death. Those who smoked more each day (or smoked for more years) had higher chances of death.

Different Causes

By doing this same kind of math, you can find the chances of dying from different causes. The graph shows which diseases killed the most people in each group.

For example, you can see that among every 100 nonsmokers who died, about 62 died of diseases of the heart and circulatory system. You can also see that for every 100 nonsmokers who died from all causes, 109 cigarette smokers died—*just from diseases of the heart and circulatory system.*

A disease that showed the greatest effect of smoking was a special kind of cancer: lung cancer. (In the graph, this disease is just part of the cancer portion.) Among the 187,783 men in the study, there were only 37 deaths by lung cancer in men who did not smoke, but 397 deaths in men who smoked cigarettes. So the chances of dying by lung cancer were more than ten times greater in smokers than in nonsmokers.

It was a surprise to find that so many diseases were affected by smoking. Many people were also surprised to learn that, all put together, the chances of death were 70 percent greater in smokers than in nonsmokers.

"I don't like to think about 'chances of death.' I just want to be well."

I understand. And I know that at your age death seems a long way off. But there is no way to measure just how well or how sick people are. And counting deaths tells a lot more than you might think. People who died of these diseases had to be sick first, sometimes for years. So "chances of death" also means "chances of not being well."

Now you know why all packages of cigarettes have some warning that smoking may injure your health.

Why Do People Smoke?

Because they get hooked as kids.

Tom started smoking three years ago, when he was sixteen years old. Four times he has tried to quit. He has not succeeded yet.

During each of his first three tries, he stayed away from cigarettes for about a week. The fourth time he quit for four months.

Scientists who study our health and habits—we can call them the "disease detectives"—are interested in people like Tom. Their records show that smoking causes more deaths than any other habit.

Author's Note: This chapter was written by my colleague, Andy Boyles. I have included it because it goes hand-in-hand with the previous chapter, "Science Looks at Smoking."

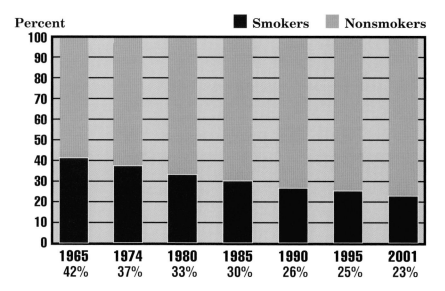

Percent						■ Smokers	▨ Nonsmokers

1965 42% **1974** 37% **1980** 33% **1985** 30% **1990** 26% **1995** 25% **2001** 23%

Adults Are Quitting, But . . .

From 1964 to 1990, the number of adult smokers in the United States dropped from 42 percent of the population to 26 percent. Since then the numbers have been going down by only 1 or 2 percent every five years. The reason: Kids are taking up the habit.

In the 1960s, the nation began a program to help people stop smoking. And between 1964 and 1990, the number of adult smokers in this country dropped about 3 percent every five years, from 42 percent of the population to 26 percent.

But since 1990, the percentage of smokers has not gone down as fast as before. Now the number is dropping by only 1 or 2 percent every five years. In 2002, the figure was between 22 and 23 percent. How can we get the size of this group to shrink even more?

Disease detectives have done studies to try to answer that question.

There are just two ways to leave the group that we call smokers: Either quit smoking or die.

The disease detectives have already shown that many smokers die younger than nonsmokers. Also, some adult smokers quit for good every year. So if everything else were to stay the same, the number of smokers should continue to go down.

54

But everything else has not stayed the same. While some smokers die and others quit, other people are starting to smoke. And most of those new smokers are young.

Kids Who Smoke

To find out how to keep kids away from cigarettes, scientists are studying young smokers.

Disease detectives at the Centers for Disease Control and Prevention have received some answers through a study called the Teenage Attitudes and Practices Survey.

In one part of the study, 9,965 teenagers and twelve-year-olds answered the scientists' questions by mail or telephone.

In answering one question, more than 38 percent of the young smokers said they thought they could stop smoking whenever they wanted.

But in answering another question, 86 percent of them said they had already tried to quit at least once. More than 75 percent of them had tried to quit in the previous six months.

Doctors and scientists say that anyone who tries to quit and then returns to smoking is probably addicted. Still, 54 percent of the smokers believed that they would quit smoking within a year.

Another part of the picture comes from a different survey, which is called Monitoring the Future.

In this survey, disease detectives at the University of Michigan have been asking questions of thousands of students across the United States every year since 1975.

In one part of the study, the scientists asked high-school seniors who smoked if they thought they would still be smoking five years later. More than half of those seniors said they would either "definitely" or "probably" quit.

The disease detectives called the same people about five years later. Nearly 60 percent were still smoking just as much as before, or even more.

Mysterious Addiction

These surveys show that many kids think cigarettes are not addictive. In fact, the drug in cigarettes, which is called nicotine, is so addictive that it has puzzled scientists.

When smokers try to quit, they may feel anxious, irritable, restless, and several other effects, which are called withdrawal symptoms. But these symptoms are not severe enough to make quitting as hard as it is.

Some scientists think the secret of nicotine's power is that it offers short-term solutions to everyday problems, such as stress.

Some smokers may not deal with stress in healthful ways, which might include breathing exercises and other ways to relax. Instead, they learn to depend on nicotine, which has a strong calming effect. According to this idea, smokers get hooked because they begin to deal with each stressful situation by smoking a cigarette.

Tom's story is an example. "I always thought that if I ever started smoking, I could quit whenever I wanted," he says.

But each time he tried to quit, he went back to smoking because it helped him deal with the stress of family disagreements or problems at school.

"I thought I would just have one," he says. "But then I was having two, and then three, and then the whole pack. I didn't want to. It just happened."

Now Tom has decided to quit again. He realizes that he might go back to smoking. He also knows that some people have succeeded in quitting. And he knows that if he ever quits trying, he will be smoking all his life.

How Fast Can You Work?

Scientists measured the horsepower of an athlete.

Eight men of the 1924 Yale rowing crew became the subject of a famous experiment. Just watching the crew in training gave the idea of the experiment to Professor Yandell Henderson. He was studying effects of exercise in athletes and helping to train the crew with his friend Howard Haggart.

Rowing can be a very heavy exercise, especially for a university crew. Eight men with long oars sit facing backward in a long slender boat, so light that it is called a racing shell. They face a ninth person, called a *coxswain,* up front who calls out the beat to keep them in time and does a little cheerleading. Each man sits on a seat that slides so he can push back with his legs each time he pulls on the oar. Then he quickly folds up his legs and pushes forward on the oar to get ready for the next pull. So each stroke uses almost all of the body's muscles, from toes to fingers. With a coxswain calling out a rhythm of up to forty strokes each minute, that's hard work.

Champion Rowers

Another reason for the experiment was the "unparalleled athletic record" of the crew. Early in the year, they won races against several universities, including Pennsylvania, Columbia, Princeton, and Cornell—some in record times. On June 13 and 14 in Olympic Trials they won two races over a 1-mile course, one at a record speed of 12.42 miles per hour. Six days later they won the annual 4-mile race against Harvard in 22 minutes. Then on the next day they sailed for France and the Olympic Games,

training as they went. After preliminaries of the Olympics, they won their final race over the 2,000-meter course by five boat lengths at a world-record time of 5 minutes and 51 seconds.

You can understand why Professor Henderson's pride in the crew was showing when he wrote: "It is doubtless true that skill, and not mere strength, wins races. But it is also highly probable that men with such a record stand virtually at the acme of dynamic efficiency." So the professor decided to use their performance as a measure of *manpower*—how fast a man can do physical work.

The next step in the experiment was to measure the power needed to propel the crew and shell at the speed of the Olympic race, which was 18.2 feet per second. To do that, the shell and crew were towed behind a motorboat at different speeds. A spring scale between the boat and towline weighed the "drawbar pull" at each speed. Naturally, when the boat went faster, the weighed amount of pull became greater. At 18.2 feet per second, the drawbar pull was measured at 110 pounds.

How Many Horses?

Now we can figure out the work actually being done in the race by the eight-man crew:

18.2 feet per second x 110 pounds=2,002 foot-pounds per second.

Then we can divide by 8 to get 250 foot-pounds per second for each man. We have done this just as an engineer would do to figure out the power of a machine. An engineer probably would go one step further and divide by 550 foot-pounds per second, the same rate of work as 1 horsepower. Doing that, we get 0.45 horsepower for a man.

There is still a problem that each rower also did some work that went into moving the boat oars. The boat moves only when each rower pulls on his oar to push backward on the water. Of course the blade of the oar slips a little in pushing water. Then each rower has to push his arms down and forward to raise the blade of the oar and get it ready for the next stroke. Probably with some engineering help, Professor Henderson figured out that in the Olympic race each man was doing work at a rate of 0.57 horsepower.

Of course, we all know that our bodies cannot keep working for long times at such high speed. (No one has measured how fast the body can work for a whole day, but it is believed to be less than 0.1 horsepower.) We can say Professor Henderson's value for a manpower is a measure of how fast a well-trained 172-pound man can do maximum physical work for a period of six minutes. Since the number cannot be exact, I think of it as one-half horsepower.

What's a Horsepower?

That was determined a long time ago, actually in 1775 at the time of the American Revolution. A Scottish inventor, James Watt, made such great improvements in the steam engine that he sometimes is called its inventor. The steam engine became a new and important source of power to grind grain, pump water, and run factories. Before that time the best source of power had been provided by horses. In order to sell his engines, Watt needed some measure of how powerful they were.

Watt measured how fast a horse could work as it usually did in pulling a load. An easy way to measure work is to see how high a weight is lifted (distance x weight), or *foot-pounds*. Since power measures how fast you do work, power can be measured as foot-pounds per second. It is said that to be safe Watt added a 50 percent extra margin and called that one horsepower. He decided on a value: 550 foot-pounds per second = 1 horsepower (HP). Today we seldom think of horses as a source of power. But we use that value of James Watt as a measure of power the world over.

BIBLIOGRAPHY

Why Do We Laugh?
Provine, R. R. 1993. Laughter punctuates speech: linguistic, social and gender contexts of laughter. *Ethology* 95:291–298.

Can You Roll Your Tongue?
Sturtevant, A. H. 1940. A new inherited character in man. *Proceedings of the National Academy of Sciences* 26: 100–102

Hsu, T. C. 1948. Tongue upfolding: a newly reported heritable character in man. *Journal of Heredity* 39:187–188.

On Top of Mount Everest
West, J. B. 1984. Human physiology at extreme altitudes on Mount Everest. *Science* 223:748–788.

West, J. B. 1986. Highest inhabitants in the world. *Nature* 324:517.

Living in Space
David, L. 1992. Artificial gravity and space travel. *BioScience* 42:155–159.

Roommates in Space
Wood, J. 1999. Psychological changes in hundred-day remote Antarctic field groups. *Environment and Behavior* 31:299–337.

Wood, J. 2000. A comparison of positive and negative experiences in Antarctic winter stations. *Environment and Behavior* 32:84–110.

Why You Can't Keep Your Eye on the Ball
Bahill, A. T., and T. LaRitz. 1984. Why can't batters keep their eyes on the ball? *American Scientist* 72:249–253.

The Sun and Your Skin
Hurwitz, S. 1988. The sun and sunscreen protection: recommendations for children. *Journal of Dermatological Surgery and Oncology* 14:657–660.

Glanz, K., M. Saraiya, and H. Wechsler. 2002. Guidelines for school programs to prevent skin cancer. *Morbidity and Mortality Weekly Report* 51(RR04): 1–16.

Science Looks at Smoking
Hammond, E. C., and D. Horn. 1958. Smoking and death rates. I. Total mortality. *Journal of the American Medical Association* 166:1159–1172.

Hammond, E. C., and D. Horn. 1958. Smoking and death rates. II. Death rates by cause. *Journal of the American Medical Association* 166:1294–1308.

Why Do People Smoke?
Allen, K. F., A. J. Moss, G. A. Giovino, D. R. Shopland, and J. P. Pierce. Teenage tobacco use. *Advance Data from Vital and Health Statistics, no. 224.* Hyattsville, Maryland: National Center for Health Statistics, 1992.

Preventing Tobacco Use Among Young People: A Report of the Surgeon General. Atlanta, Georgia: U.S. Department of Health and Human Services, 1994.

How Fast Can You Work?
Henderson, Y., and H. Haggard, 1924. The maximum human power. *American Journal of Physiology* 72:264–282.

INDEX